Sabrina Carpenter

A Little Golden Book® Biography

By Cat Reynolds • Illustrated by Beverly Johnson

A GOLDEN BOOK • NEW YORK
Golden Books
An imprint of Random House Children's Books
A division of Penguin Random House LLC
1745 Broadway, New York, NY 10019
penguinrandomhouse.com
rhcbooks.com

Library of Congress Control Number: 2025938041
ISBN 979-8-217-22435-7 (trade) — ISBN 979-8-217-22436-4 (ebook)
Manufactured in the United States of America
10 9 8 7 6 5 4 3 2 1
The authorized representative in the EU for product safety and compliance is Penguin Random House Ireland, Morrison Chambers, 32 Nassau Street, Dublin D02 YH68, Ireland.
https://eu-contact.penguin.ie

Sabrina Annlynn Carpenter was born on May 11, 1999, in Quakertown, Pennsylvania. She grew up in East Greenville with her parents and three older sisters, Cayla, Shannon, and Sarah.

When she was little, Sabrina loved to sing and dance for her family. She knew from a very young age that she wanted to be a star.

Sabrina enjoyed years of dance classes, beginning with ballet when she was just two years old. She also learned hip-hop, jazz, and tap dancing.

She started taking singing lessons when she was six. A few years later, Sabrina began making videos of herself performing songs by her favorite artists, like Taylor Swift and Miley Cyrus. She entered one of her videos in a national singing competition and came in third place out of 7,000 entries!

Sabrina's parents were happy to help their youngest daughter follow her dreams. Her father turned a closet in their home into a recording studio. It was the perfect place for Sabrina to practice singing.

Singing and dancing aren't Sabrina's only talents. She is also an actor. At the age of twelve, she had her first role on a TV show.

The next year, Sabrina and her mom moved to Los Angeles so that she could focus on her career. She auditioned for more TV shows and movies and kept getting new parts.

In 2014, Sabrina got her big break: a starring role in the Disney Channel comedy *Girl Meets World*. She played Maya Hart, a free-spirited middle-school student and the best friend of the main character, Riley Matthews. The show ran for three seasons.

Even while she was busy acting on *Girl Meets World*, Sabrina kept writing and recording music. Soon before her fifteenth birthday, she released her first single, "Can't Blame a Girl for Trying." A year later, her first album, *Eyes Wide Open*, came out.

Sabrina's sister Sarah was a backup singer on the album and can also be seen singing in the music video for the title song.

Sabrina worked hard on her career, but she still made sure to spend time with her sisters. The four girls like to share clothes, help each other get ready for big events, visit new places together, and have sleepovers.

Sabrina looks up to her sisters and loves knowing that they're always there for her.

When Sabrina was seventeen, she went on tour to promote her second album, *Evolution*. She loved performing in front of fans in cities across the country. Soon she released two more albums, *Singular: Act I* and *Singular: Act II*.

Sabrina continued to take on more acting roles. Each project allowed her to try something new. She played a serious character in the movie *The Hate U Give*. She was the lead in the film *Work It* as well as an executive producer. And she had the opportunity to perform on Broadway in the musical *Mean Girls*.

Sabrina cowrites a lot of her music. In 2021, "Skin" became her first song to make it onto the music charts. Her next album, *Emails I Can't Send*, featured two more hit singles, "Nonsense" and "Feather." Sabrina's music was being heard by more people than ever before.

One person who especially loved Sabrina's songs was Taylor Swift. They met for the first time in 2017. The two pop stars had a lot in common and became good friends.

In 2023, Taylor asked Sabrina to open for her on her Eras Tour. Sabrina was now performing in front of thousands of people around the world!

By 2024, there was no doubt that Sabrina Carpenter was a star! That year, she was the musical guest on an episode of the popular TV show *Saturday Night Live*. She attended the Met Gala charity event at New York's Metropolitan Museum of Art, and she performed at the Coachella music festival.

At Coachella, Sabrina sang "Espresso," a song from her album *Short n' Sweet*. Some people think the title of the album describes the petite singer, who is exactly five feet tall.

"Espresso" became Sabrina's first song to make it to the top of the charts. She wouldn't have to wait long to have more big hits, though. The next three singles from *Short n' Sweet* were also number one songs.

Sabrina was now an international pop star! She's played in sold-out arenas across North America and Europe. Her fans around the world love singing along with her.

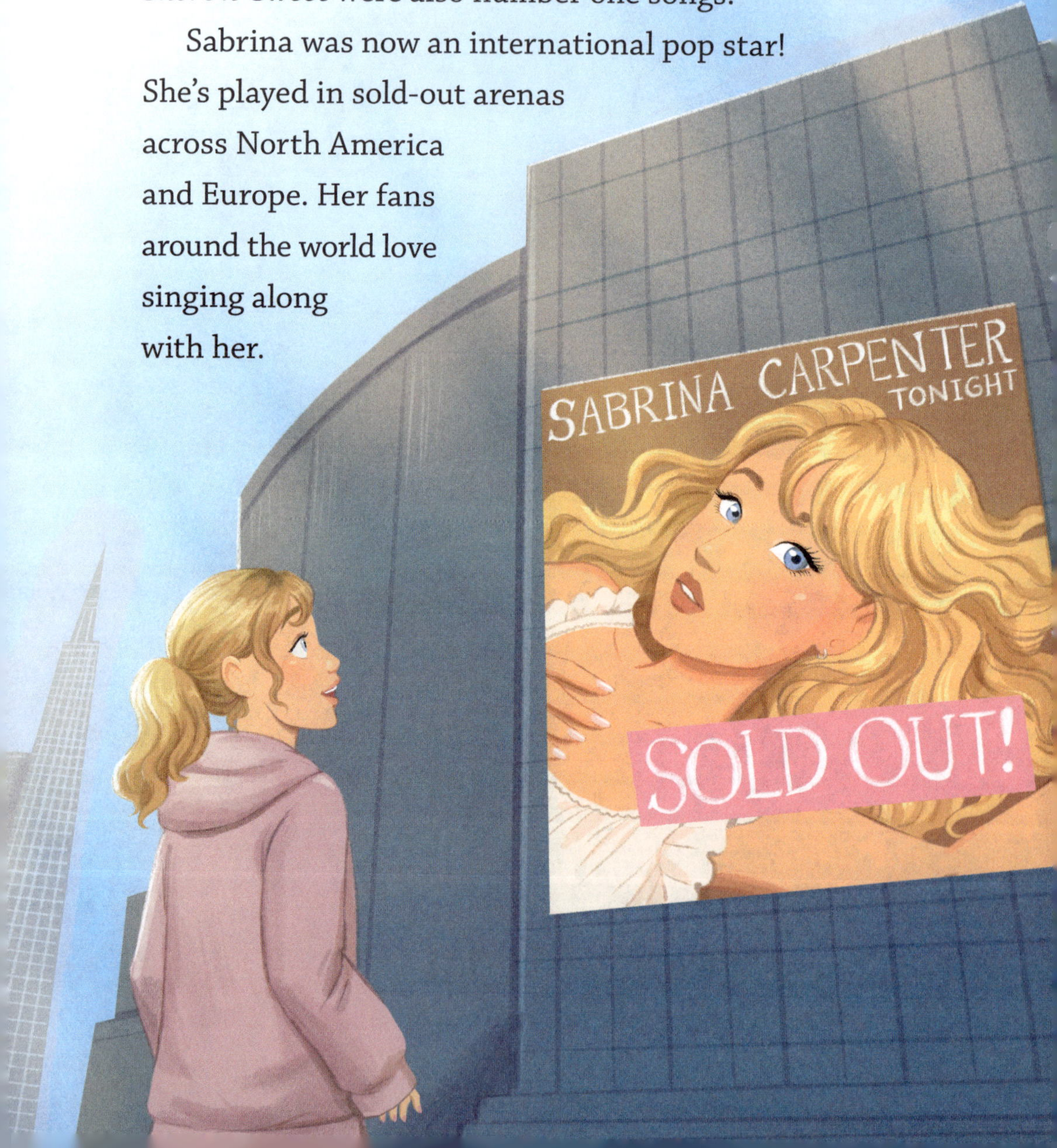

In 2025, Sabrina was honored to receive two Grammys. She won the award for Best Pop Vocal Album and for Best Pop Solo Performance.

Sabrina never forgot the support she had from her family. "I want to thank my mom for driving me to every voice lesson," she said during her acceptance speech. "And I want to thank my dad and my sisters."

Sabrina uses her fame to support important causes she believes in. On her Short n' Sweet Tour, young concertgoers were given the opportunity to register to vote. She also created the Sabrina Carpenter Fund to support mental health awareness, animal welfare, and LGBTQ+ rights.

When Sabrina isn't working, she likes to draw, play with her dogs, and go to fitness classes with her friends. She also enjoys spending time at home with her prized possession: her piano. Songwriting isn't just about creating her next big hit—for Sabrina, it's also a way to understand her own feelings and learn about herself.

Sabrina Carpenter never gave up on her dream of being a star. With hard work, dedication, and support from her family, she knew anything was possible.

Today, Sabrina is an award-winning singer, songwriter, and actor who inspires others to dream big and reach for the stars!